PHILLIES FUN AND GAMES

A Trivial Account of Phillies History

LANA BANDY AND
DALE RATERMANN

Blue River Press

Cover designed by Phil Velikan
Cover photo by arrangement with AP photos
Proofread by Dorothy Chambers
Packaged by Wish Publishing

Printed in the United States of America
10 9 8 7 6 5 4 3 2 1

Distributed in the United States by
Cardinal Publishers Group
www.cardinalpub.com

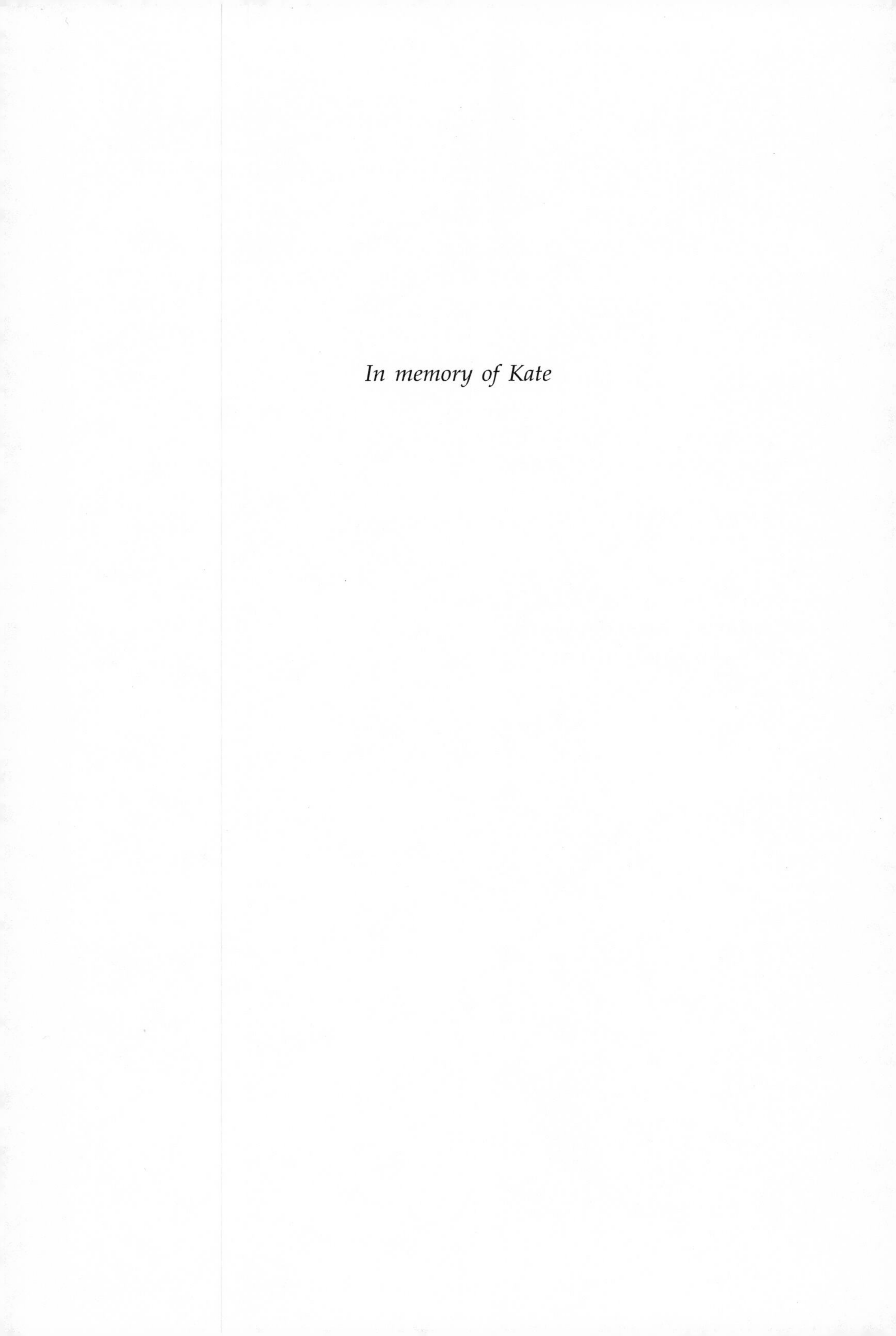

In memory of Kate

TABLE OF CONTENTS

Authors Note... 7

2008 Phillies... 9

History... 31

Retired Uniform Numbers... 51

Hitters... 60

Pitchers... 70

Managers... 79

Stadiums... 83

Answers... 87

Bibliography... 104

AUTHORS' NOTE

There's no more appropriate way to celebrate the Philadelphia Phillies' 2008 World Series championship than to cherish the past. And the Phillies' past is checkered with colorful characters, wonderful stories and great accomplishments.

This collection of trivia and puzzles will test your knowledge of the Phillies, past and present, as well as provide you with hours of entertainment.

Designed for fans of all ages, the puzzles are standard crosswords and word searches with various difficulty levels, as well as take-offs of the popular Sudoku and Cryptoquip puzzles.

There are instructions where necessary. All the answers can be found at the back of the book.

So grab a pencil, sit back and relax as you relive the Phillies' history and 2008 world championship.

2008 PHILLIES

The Phillies had a dream season in 2008. For just the second time in franchise history, the Phillies won the World Series, beating the Tampa Bay Rays, four games to one. The team won the National League East Championship with a 92-70 record. It was the team's second consecutive division title and the sixth consecutive winning season.

The '08 Phillies were led by Ryan Howard's major league-leading 48 HR and 146 RBI. Other standouts included Jimmy Rollins (.277 BA, 47 SB) and Chase Utley (.292 BA, 33 HR, 104 RBI). The top pitchers were Jamie Moyer (16-7), Cole Hamels (14-10) and closer Brad Lidge (41 saves, 1.95 ERA).

Philadelphia consistenly racked up wins all year, including a crucial seven in a row in September. They went into the playoffs having won 13 of their last 16 regular-season games.

The Phillies beat the Milwaukee Brewers in the division series and the Los Angeles Dodgers in the NL Championship series to set up their second World Series title.

PHILLIES PHACTS

Birthplaces of Players, 2008 Team

Pedro Feliz – Dominican Republic

Tadahito Iguchi – Japan

J.C. Romero – Puerto Rico

Carlos Ruiz – Panama

Matt Stairs – Canada

So Taguchi – Japan

2008 PLAYERS

Match each player who appeared in the 2008 postseason with the fact about him.

Hitters

1. Eric Bruntlett ____
2. Pat Burrell ____
3. Chris Coste ____
4. Greg Dobbs ____
5. Pedro Feliz ____
6. Ryan Howard ____
7. Geoff Jenkins ____
8. Jimmy Rollins ____
9. Carlos Ruiz ____
10. Matt Stairs ____
11. So Taguchi ____
12. Chase Utley ____
13. Shane Victorino ____
14. Jayson Werth ____

Hitter Facts

a. Set the franchise record with 27 HBP in 2008.

b. Played for Panama in the inaugural World Baseball Classic.

c. One of nine major league players to have 20 HR and 20 SB in 2008.

d. Appeared in several MC Hammer and Mavis Staples music videos.

e. Set a Phillies record with 22 pinch-hits in 2008.

f. Has appeared in major league games at C, 1B, 3B, SS and OF.

g. Graduated from Stanford with a degree in economics.

h. Won the 2006 Media Good Guy Award from the Philadelphia Sportswriters Association.

i. Ended 2008 with 277 consecutive games played, the longest streak among active players.

j. Hit a HR in his major league debut with Milwaukee in 1998.

k. Was the No. 1 pick in the 1998 major league draft.

l. Acquired from the Blue Jays in 2008 for Fabio Castro.

m. Born and raised in Hawaii.

n. Was a teammate of Ichiro Suzuki on the Orix Blue Wave.

Answers on page 87.

Pitchers

1. Joe Blanton ____
2. Clay Condrey ____
3. Chad Durbin ____
4. Scott Eyre ____
5. Cole Hamels ____
6. J.A. Happ ____
7. Brad Lidge ____
8. Ryan Madson ____
9. Jamie Moyer ____
10. Brett Myers ____
11. J.C. Romero ____

PHILLIES PHACTS

MOST HOME RUNS, MAJOR LEAGUES, 2006-08

153, Ryan Howard
124, Alex Rodriguez
120, Adam Dunn
118, Albert Pujols
112, Prince Fielder
112, David Ortiz

Pitcher Facts

a. Had a career-high 15 SO at Cincinnati on 4/21/07.

b. Was the losing pitcher in the 2008 major league All-Star Game.

c. Was starter on Opening Day 2008 at the Tokyo Dome.

d. Named No. 1 MLB Good Guy in 2004 by *The Sporting News*.

e. Threw the first pitch (as the starter) and last pitch (as the closer) of the Phils' 2007 regular season.

f. Led all NL relievers in IP in 2008.

g. Pitched for the Twins, Angels and Red Sox before joining the Phils in 2007.

h. Was a combined 5-0 in 2008 with the Phillies and Cubs.

i. Traded to Philadelphia for Trino Aguilar in 2004.

j. Set a Phillies record in 2004 by not allowing an earned run in the first 21 innings of his career.

k. Won the 2008 Paul Owens Award as the best pitcher in the Phils' minor league system.

Answers on page 87.

2008 PLAYERS

ACROSS

1. Runs ahead by
3. Nixes, NASA style
9. Named NL Player of the Month for September in 2007 & '08 ☆
11. River transportation
12. TV show: *American* ___
14. Was 3rd in NL with 34 infield hits in '08 ☆
17. Mariners' home
18. Has had 8 consecutive seasons of 20+ HR ☆
21. Santa's helper
23. Possess
26. P acquired from Cubs in August deal ☆
27. Phils' 1st round pick in 2002 draft ☆
28. 1B + 2*2B + 3*3B + 4*HR
31. Tardy
32. Started 92 games behind the plate☆
33. Only 3rd Japanese player to start a World Series game (2004) ☆
36. Sub. batter

37. Demands
39. Semi radio, often
41. J.A. Happ's coll. ☆
43. Wore uniform No. 63 ☆
45. Finish
46. Force out of office
47. Tigers' Kaline
48. Japanese currency
49. Skyscraper's people mover
51. Scorecard notation for swiping second
52. Night before a holiday
54. Pitcher's stat
55. Opening Day starter ☆
56. Set club record with 22 pinch hits ☆
57. Go by plane

DOWN

2. Carlos' goodbye
4. P acquired from Oakland in July deal ☆
5. Cab
6. Fancy pitcher
7. Filled in at SS during Rollins' disabled list stint ☆
8. Scorecard notation for a walk
9. Fedora, e.g.
10. Was 41-for-41 in save opportunities in '08 ☆
13. Allow
14. Day that marked the end of WWII
15. Computer brains, for short
16. Boat propeller
19. 2007 NL MVP ☆
20. Former
22. Won August game with 3-run 11th-inning walk-off HR vs. Dodgers ☆
23. Either's partner
24. Grandson of former major leaguer Dick Schofield ☆
25. No-no (var.)
29. Wagers
30. Farm machinery
31. Buried
34. One of central figures in a Stephen King novel ☆
35. Slangy hello
36. School outdoor activities class (init.)
38. Reynolds Wrap product (var.)
40. LHP J.C. ☆
41. Government org. that produces foreign intelligence info
42. He homered in five consecutive games in 2008, twice ☆
43. Oldest player on the team, at 45 ☆
44. Relief pitchers' stats
50. Science experiment room
53. Stock symbol for Veolia Environn Ads
54. Phils Bouchee ☆

Answers on page 87.

2008 SEASON

1. Which two Phillies had the team's longest consecutive-game hitting streak of 14?

2. Who were the only two Phils pitchers who hurled a complete game?

3. Who was the oldest player on the team?

4. Who were the only three players to catch at least one game for the Phils?

5. Did the Phillies have a better record in home games or road games?

6. Which team scored 14 runs in one game against the Phils in 2008?

7. Who was the only Phillies player to hit three home runs in a game?

8. What was the Phils' longest winning streak of the season?

9. What was the Phils' longest losing streak of the season?

10. True or False? The Phils' .255 team batting average was 10th best in the NL.

11. Who were the two NL players who joined Pat Burrell (102) as the only ones with 100+ walks in '08?

12. Who led the team in extra base hits, Ryan Howard or Chase Utley?

13. Who led the Phils in sacrifice bunts with 12?

14. Who was the only NL pitcher with a lower opponents' batting average than Cole Hamels' .227?

15. After going 92-70 in '08, how many consecutive seasons have the Phillies had a winning record?

16. True or False? The Phillies were 79-0 when they had a lead after eight innings.

17. Which two Phils finished first and second in the NL in stolen base percentage?

18. How many consecutive games did the Phillies hit a home run in '08 to set a franchise record?

19. True or False? The Phillies led the major leagues with 214 home runs.

20. Which Phils pitcher won the most road games in '08?

21. Among the regulars, who had the highest batting average with runners in scoring position?

22. True or False? The Phils' home attendance total of 3,422,583 in '08 was a club record.

23. Which pitcher tied for the NL lead in hit batsmen, with 14?

24. The NL average for relief pitching ERA was 4.09. Were the Phils above or below that figure?

25. The NL batting average for pinch-hitters was .229. Were the Phils above or below that figure?

Answers on page 88.

RYAN HOWARD

1. Where did Ryan attend college?

2. When Ryan won *The Sporting News'* Player of the Year Award in 2006, who finished second in the balloting?

3. Who is the only major league player in his second season to have more RBIs than Ryan's 149 in his "sophomore" season of 2006?

4. Ryan became the fastest player to hit 100 HR in his career (325 games). Whose major league record did he break?

5. What is Ryan's middle name?

6. True or False? Howard is the first player in history to lead the NL in HR and RBIs while winning the pennant and not be named the league's Most Valuable Player (in 2008).

7. True or False? Howard is the first player in history to be leading his league in HR and RBI at the All-Star break and not make the All-Star team (in 2008).

8. Ryan became only the second Phillies player with 30 HR and 100 RBI in three consecutive seasons. Who is the other player to accomplish that?

9. In his major league career, does Ryan have a higher batting average against RHP or LHP?

10. Entering the 2009 season, which NL team has Ryan hit the most HR against?

Answers on page 88.

HOWARD-DO-KU PUZZLE

Use logic to fill in the boxes so that every row, column and 2x3 box contains the letters H-O-W-A-R-D.

	W	R	A		
R		D	O	W	
	O	W	R		D
		O	H	D	

W					A
			D		H
O	A				
				A	W
R		A			
H					R

		O			R
		D	W		O
		H			A
R			D		
W		A	O		
O			A		

Answers on page 89.

JIMMY ROLLINS

1. In which round of the major league draft did the Phillies select Jimmy in 1996?

2. How many major league All-Star Games has Jimmy played in?

3. He set a Phillies club record in 2008 for most consecutive stolen bases without being caught stealing. What is the record?

4. Is Jimmy's longest consecutive-game hitting streak more or less than 35 games?

5. True or False? He has never hit an inside-the-park home run.

6. Before Jimmy won the NL MVP Award in 2007, who was the last NL shortstop to win?

7. True or False? Jimmy has never played anywhere but shortstop for the Phillies.

8. He had 20 or more doubles, triples, home runs and stolen bases in 2007. Name one of the other three players to accomplish that feat in a single season.

JIMMY ROLLINS' CAREER BATTING AVERAGE, MONTH BY MONTH

.200, March

.271, April

.270, May

.273, June

.276, July

.277, August

.293, September

.348, October

9. Whose major league record for most at-bats in a season (716) did Jimmy break in 2007?

10. When he hit his 62nd career HR in 2006, he set the Phillies club record for most HR by a shortstop. Who held the record?

Answers on page 90.

CHASE UTLEY

1. Chase is one of three Phillies with 200 hits and 30 HR in the same season (2006). Name one of the other two players to accomplish that feat.

2. Where did Chase earn All-America honors in college?

3. True or False? Chase's first major league hit was a grand slam HR.

4. When Chase was promoted to the Phillies full-time in August 2003, whom did he replace at 2B?

5. True or False? Chase was the last batter in the last game at Veterans Stadium in 2003.

6. Chase had 100+ RBI in four consecutive seasons (2005-08). Only two other 2B have accomplished that feat in major league history. Who are they?

7. How old did Chase become when he celebrated his birthday on Dec. 17, 2008?

8. Chase spent a month in 2007 on the disabled list. What was his injury?

9. True or False? Entering the 2009 season, Chase had a higher career batting average at home than on the road.

10. Which major league team drafted Chase in the second round of the 1997 draft, but was unable to sign him?

Answers on pages 90-91 .

BRAD LIDGE'S SINGLE GAME HIGHS, CAREER

Longest Outing: 3.0 innings

Strikeouts: 6

Walks: 5

Winning Streak: 5

Losing Streak: 5

Scoreless Streak: 21.0 innings

MANAGER CHARLIE MANUEL

Phillies Manager Charlie Manuel has been with the Phillies since 2003. He became manager in 2004 after spending the time before that as special assistant to General Manager Ed Wade. Manuel led the Phillies to back-to-back division championships in 2007 and 2008, and is No. 6 on the Phillies all-time winning percentage list (.546).

Prior to working with the Phillies, Manuel spent time in the major and minor leagues as a manager and player. He managed the Cleveland Indians from 2000 to 2002, leading the team to the Central Division title in his second year. He started his coaching career as a scout for the Minnesota Twins, the team that signed him to his first professional contract.

1. Which other major league team did Charlie manage?

2. Who is the only other Phillies manager to lead the team to back-to-back division championships?

3. Which major league team hired Charlie for his first non-playing job in baseball?

4. Which two major league teams did Charlie play for?

5. Who were the two managers he played for in the major leagues?

6. True or False? As a minor league player in the Midwest League, Charlie won the Triple Crown.

7. Charlie played for the Yakult Swallows and Kintetsu Buffaloes from 1976-81. In which league do the Swallows and Buffaloes play?

8. Does Charlie bat right- or left-handed?

9. Does Charlie throw right- or left-handed?

10. Where does he live in the off-season?

Answers on page 91.

2008 COACHES

Match each coach on the 2008 team with his primary responsibility:

1. Mick Billmeyer
2. Rich Dubee
3. Ramon Henderson
4. Davey Lopes
5. Steve Smith
6. Milt Thompson
7. Jimy Williams

a. Bench Coach
b. Bullpen Coach
c. Catching Instructor
d. First Base Coach
e. Hitting Coach
f. Pitching Coach
g. Third Base Coach

Answers on page 91.

PHILLIES PHACTS

SHANE VICTORINO'S BATTING AVERAGE BREAKDOWN, CAREER

.409, vs. Pittsburgh

.091, vs. Baltimore (1-11) and Texas (1-11)

.500, at McAfee Coliseum (5-10)

.000, at Rogers Centre (0-10)

.284, on grass

.000, on artificial turf (0-15)

.281, at home

.281, on the road

2008 WORLD SERIES

1. On what day of the week was Game 1 played?

2. Who hit a two-run homer in the top of the first inning of Game 1 to give the Phillies a 2-0 lead?

3. Who was the Phillies winning pitcher in Game 1?

4. What is the name of the Rays' home ballpark that hosted Games 1 and 2?

5. Who hit a home run in Game 2 and scored the winning run in Game 3?

6. Who drove in the winning run of Game 3 with the World Series' first "walkoff" infield single?

7. Name two of the three Phils who homered in Game 3.

8. Which Phils pitcher homered in Game 4, the first pitcher to hit a World Series HR since 1974? (He also was the winning pitcher.)

9. True or False? Games 3 and 4 were played on the same day.

10. What inning was it when Game 5 was suspended?

11. Who was the winning pitcher of Game 5, and who picked up the save?

12. True or False? Game 5 was the first World Series contest that was suspended.

13. Which TV network televised the game and who were the lead announcers?

14. Who was named the MVP of the Series?

15. What is the official name of the World Series trophy, and who makes it?

Answers on page 91.

PHILLIES PHACTS

MOST RBI BY MAJOR LEAGUE SECOND BASEMEN, 2005-08

404, Chase Utley

301, Robinson Cano

297, Jeff Kent

269, Dan Uggla

253, Ray Durham

MINOR LEAGUE TEAMS

Match the Phillies' minor league team cities with the team's nickname and team's league in 2008.

1. Clearwater ____ ____
2. Lakewood ____ ____
3. Lehigh Valley ____ ____
4. Reading ____ ____
5. Williamsport ____ ____

A. Blueclaws

B. Crosscutters

C. Ironpigs

D. Phillies

E. Threshers

a. Eastern (AA)

b. Florida State (A)

c. International (AAA)

d. NY-Penn (A)

e. South Atlantic (A)

Answers on page 91.

HISTORY

The Phillies have a long and interesting baseball history. While the team proudly won two World Series championships (2008 and 1980), they have also struggled at times. The Phillies have lost more games than any other team in Major League baseball.

In the late 1800s, Alfred J. Reach, a Philadelphia sporting goods store owner, bought the team that was to become the Phillies. The Phillies started play in 1883, making them one of the oldest franchises in U.S. professional sports. The team's first game was against the Providence Grays. The Phillies lost 4-3 at Recreation Park (24th and Columbia Avenues). The team went 17-81-1 that season, finishing last in the league.

The Phillies shared fans with the American League's Philadelphia A's in the first half of the 1900s. The A's, under manager Connie Mack, were more successful than the Phillies, winning six pennants in their first 15 years, but the team moved to Kansas City in 1954.

The Phillies' first taste of success came in 1915 when they won the pennant. The team was led by the pitching of Grover Cleveland Alexander and the hitting of Gavvy Cravath. That year, Cravath set the single-season home run record with 24. The Phillies eventually lost the World Series to the Boston Red Sox.

The team hit hard times after that, with just one winning season in the 30 years from 1918 to 1948.

The 1950 season was a bright spot for Philadelphia. The Phillies team, nicknamed the Whiz Kids, won the pennant that year. The team was led by future Hall of Famers Richie Ashburn and Robin Roberts. One of the most exciting games that season was the last one of the year versus the Dodgers. Dick Sisler hit a three-run homer in the 10th inning to clinch the pennant for Philadelphia, 4-1. The Phillies ended up losing the championship to the New York Yankees that season.

The Phillies were mediocre for the rest of the 1950s. The team hovered around the .500 mark but never finished above third in the National League. The most notable streak in the 1960s (the Gene Mauch era) came in 1964. The team had a six-and-a-half-game lead before suffering a 10-game losing streak. They ended up losing the pennant by one game to the

St. Louis Cardinals. Now known as the "Phold of '64," it's one of the most memorable collapses in U.S. sports history.

The 1970s started poorly, but ended strong. Under manager Danny Ozark, the Phillies won three consecutive NL East Division Championships from 1976 to 1978, but they could not get a World Series title. One memorable time during the decade was when Phillie Phanatic, the team's furry green mascot, debuted in 1978.

The team's luck changed in 1980. Pitcher Steve Carlton, along with outfielder Greg Luzinski and infielders Mike Schmidt, Larry Bowa and Pete Rose, led the Phillies to the World Series title.

It was a memorable league series versus Houston, with four of the five games going into extra innings. A Garry Maddox hit in the 10th inning gave the Phillies their first pennant in 30 years.

The tough-fought World Series title came in game six vs. Kansas City. Tug McGraw struck out KC's Willie Wilson for the victory. Schmidt, the National League MVP, also became the World Series MVP after hitting 8-for-21 (.381).

The Phillies made it to the World Series again in 1983 but lost to the Baltimore Orioles, four games to one. The Phillies had just one season above .500 over the next decade, finishing second in 1986.

The team won nearly 60% of its games in 1993, when Manager Jim Fregosi led the team past the Atlanta Braves for the National League pennant. The Toronto Blue Jays defeated Philadelphia in the World Series.

Philadelphia had its first winning season in eight years in 2001 under new Manager Larry Bowa. Bowa led the team for nearly four seasons before Charlie Manuel took the reins. Manuel has led the team to winning seasons every year. The 2007 team won the East pennant (but lost the Division Series to the Colorado Rockies), and the 2008 team, of course, won the World Series.

When the Phillies win, they win big. The team has experienced numerous ups and downs throughout the years – one of the things that makes being a Philadelphia Phillies fan so much fun.

1. Name the Phils second baseman acquired from the Cubs in 1960 who made the NL All-Star team that season.

2. What's the longest game the Phillies ever played?

3. Who was the Phils general manager who retired following the 2008 season?

4. Who was the Phils new general manager for the 2009 season?

5. Which two regulars on the 2008 team were acquired through free agency?

6. Who was the highest paid player on the '08 team?

7. True or False? The Phillies are the only pro sports team in any league with more than 10,000 losses.

8. Who has played more games at first base than any player in Phillies history?

9. Who was the last Phillies starting outfielder to go an entire season without committing an error?

MAJOR LEAGUE TEAMS

Y	C	T	E	S	U	A	B	R	E	W	E	R	S	S
J	H	L	V	K	I	A	S	T	R	O	S	D	H	E
S	S	M	M	C	S	I	N	D	I	A	N	S	A	R
M	R	S	A	A	E	L	S	E	T	A	R	I	P	D
T	E	E	N	B	S	L	A	N	I	D	R	A	C	A
F	G	L	G	D	S	R	E	N	I	R	A	M	S	P
M	D	O	E	N	S	A	E	S	O	R	E	D	S	P
Z	O	I	L	O	A	Y	S	G	T	I	D	D	G	H
Y	D	R	S	M	M	R	A	X	I	E	T	B	I	I
R	A	O	E	A	B	C	E	J	O	T	M	A	A	L
A	S	N	I	I	W	H	I	T	E	S	O	X	N	L
Y	N	S	K	D	L	V	H	P	N	U	D	Z	T	I
S	I	B	C	E	S	L	A	Y	O	R	L	E	S	E
L	W	U	O	S	E	V	A	R	B	T	N	B	R	S
X	T	C	R	Z	M	S	M	A	R	L	I	N	S	B

ANGELS
A's
ASTROS
BLUE JAYS
BRAVES
BREWERS
CARDINALS
CUBS
DIAMONDBACKS
DODGERS
GIANTS
INDIANS
MARINERS
MARLINS
METS
NATIONALS
ORIOLES
PADRES
PHILLIES
PIRATES
RANGERS
RAYS
RED SOX
REDS
ROCKIES
ROYALS
TIGERS
TWINS
WHITE SOX
YANKEES

Answers on page 92.

10. Which Phillies catcher was the son of a major league All-Star and the father of two major league All-Stars?

11. Phils announcer Harry Kalas said, "Two-thirds of the Earth is covered by water, the other one-third is covered by ____." Who was Kalas referring to?

12. Which former Phils catcher maintains "that the universe is created and sustained by numerical synchronicities, and that all matter is charged with vibrational energy, which has escaped human perception because it is extradimensional in origin."

13. Who did the Phillies trade with Doug Nickle to the Cardinals in 2002 for Plácido Polanco, Mike Timlin and Bud Smith?

14. Who was the Phillies second baseman who had an unassisted triple play in 1992?

15. What young country music singer used to sing the National Anthem for the Reading Phillies?

16. Who won a Gold Glove at shortstop for the Phillies in 1963?

17. What year did the Phillie Phanatic make his debut?

18. Who was in the Phillie Phanatic costume for the first 16 years?

19. Who joined the Phillies first: Harry Kalas or the Phillie Phanatic?

20. What is the Phillies' flagship radio station?

21. What is the name of the Phillies' spring training stadium in Clearwater, Fla.?

22. Which Phillies infielder was named the MVP of the NL Championship Series in 1980?

23. Who was the Phils catcher whose father was the first nonwhite player for the Detroit Tigers?

24. Which Phils pitcher also played for the Detroit Pistons in the NBA?

25. Who was the Phils infielder diagnosed with testicular cancer during the 1994 spring training camp after three consecutive all-star seasons?

Answers on page 92.

ROOKIES IN THE ALL-STAR GAME

Del Ennis, 1946 (OF)
Richie Ashburn, 1948 (OF)
Jack Sanford, 1957 (P)
Ray Culp, 1963 (P)
Juan Samuel, 1984 (2B)
Tyler Green, 1995 (P)
Jimmy Rollins, 2001 (SS)

ROOKIES

1. Who was named by *The Sporting News* as the major league Rookie of the Year in 1946?

2. Who was the Phils NL Rookie of the Year in 1964?

3. Which Phils rookie had the most home runs in a season?

4. Who was the last Phillies player to hit a home run in his first major leagu at bat?

5. What is Pinky Whitney's club record set in 1928 for RBI in a season by a rookie?

6. Which Phils speedster set the team record by stealing 72 bases in his rookie season?

7. Who was the rookie pitcher who appeared in 65 games for the Phils in 1961?

8. Which Phils rookie pitcher in 1963 threw five shutouts?

9. Who was the catcher who broke into the Major Leagues in 1994 and wound up catching more games for the Phillies than anyone in history?

10. Who is the only Phillies rookie to play in all 162 games in his first season?

Answers on page 93.

PHILLIES PHACTS

PHILLIES TOP TEN MOST GAMES PLAYED, CAREER

1. Mike Schmidt	2,404
2. Richie Ashburn	1,794
3. Larry Bowa	1,739
4. Tony Taylor	1,669
5. Del Ennis	1,630
6. Ed Delahanty	1,544
7. Sherry Magee	1,521
8. Willie Jones	1,520
9. Granny Hamner	1,501
10. Cy Williams	1,463

BASEBALL HALL OF FAME

Which of these men enshrined in the National Baseball Hall of Fame played with the Phillies?

1. Sparky Anderson
2. Johnny Evers
3. Jimmy Foxx
4. Ferguson Jenkins
5. Nap Lajoie
6. Joe Morgan
7. Tony Perez
8. Ryne Sandberg
9. Casey Stengel
10. Hack Wilson

Answers on page 93.

WHO AM I?

How many statements does it take you to identify these former Phillies players?

1. I led the NL in triples one season (before joining the Phils).
2. I had two stints with the Phillies in the 1970s.
3. I was a left-handed hitting catcher.
4. I'm now an analyst on FOX Sports television broadcasts.

I am ______________________________

1. I played second base.
2. I hit a HR in the 10th inning to beat the Giants, 1-0, in a 1986 game.
3. I was selected to play in the 1984 All-Star Game, the same season I was named NL Rookie of the Year.
4. I was inducted into the Phillies Wall of Fame in 2008.

I am ______________________________

Answers on page 93.

WHAT'S YOUR NAME?

These Phillies had unusual names or nicknames. See how many former Phillies you can identify from reading just the first name or nickname. If you need help, match the nicknames with the surnames that follow.

1. Schoolboy	a. Beck
2. Gavvy	b. Bransfield
3. Cookie	c. Burgess
4. Bucky	d. Caballero
5. Choo Choo	e. Coleman
6. Babe	f. Cravath
7. Klondike	g. Dahlgren
8. Kitty	h. Davis
9. Monk	i. Douglass
10. Smoky	j. Dubiel
11. Pretzels	k. Edwards
12. Kiddo	l. Elliott
13. Doc	m. Fryman
14. Granny	n. Hamner
15. Greasy	o. Lowrey
16. Skinny	p. Lyle
17. Ugueth	q. McGraw
18. Pinky	r. Neale
19. Woodie	s. O'Neal
20. Tug	t. Pezzullo
21. Boom Boom	u. Rojas
22. Sparky	v. Rowe
23. Putsy	w. Urbina
24. Ace	x. Walters
25. Peanuts	y. Whitney

Answers on page 93.

ALL-STAR CROSSWORD

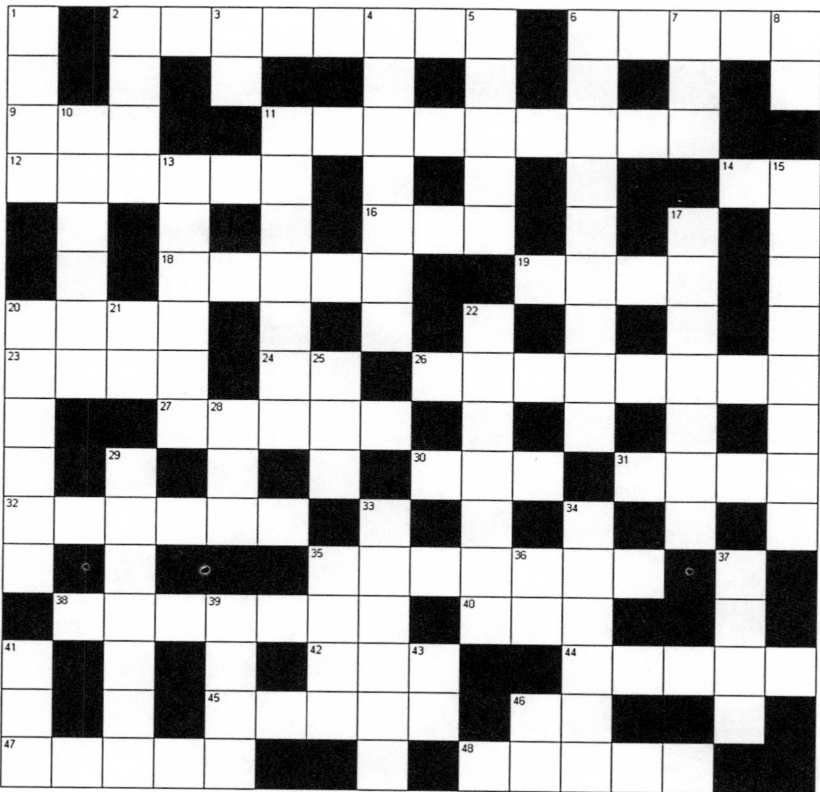

ACROSS

2. Made assurances
6. First Phillies player to participate in the HR Derby (in 2004) ☆
9. First-day stock (init.)
11. Last Phillies P to start an All-Star Game ☆
12. Phils catcher selected to 1985 team ☆
14. MLB's jr. circuit
16. Slick
18. Sped
19. Sailor's greeting
20. Brand with an alligator logo
23. Military alliance est. in 1949
24. "___ way or the highway!"
26. Hit game-winning HR in 1964 All-Star Game ☆
27. Peace prize name
30. Had goulash
31. Rough trip

32. Lemon-lime drink
35. Phils LHP named to seven all-star squads ☆
38. Difficult situation
40. A moo
42. Brooks & Dunn, e.g.
44. Winner of HR Derby at 2005 All-Star Game ☆
45. NL manager in 1981 All-Star Game ☆
46. Word on a desk box
47. Hotel prices
48. Losing pitcher in 2008 All-Star Game ☆

DOWN

1. Israeli city Tel ___
2. Needy
3. Either's partner
4. Voted starter on 1989 All-Star team despite earlier retirement ☆
5. Broadway musical: "Hello, ___"
6. RHP chosen to 1973 NL squad ☆
7. Web address ending, often
8. Former
10. MVP of 1996 All-Star Game played in Philadelphia ☆
11. Winning pitcher of 1995 All-Star Game ☆
13. RHP who was named to All-Star teams while playing for Colorado, Houston and Pittsburgh ☆
15. Phillies OF who homered in the 1977 All-Star Game ☆
17. Voted as starting OF in 1990 and '94 and '95 ☆
20. Put your money to work
21. Extra period (abbr.)
22. Starting NL SS in first game in 1933 ☆
25. Japanese currency
28. Ump's call
29. Side support on an airplane seat
33. Rookie 2B selected to play in 1984 game ☆
34. Phils OF chosen to 2007 NL squad ☆
35. Surrender possession
36. Go ___ guy
37. Evened the score
39. Behaves like a dog
41. Auto
43. Light switch setting
46. Roman 2

Answers on page 93.

BROTHERS WHO PLAYED ON THE SAME TEAM

Bennett, Dave and Dennis (1964)

Chiozza, Dino and Lou (1935)

Delahanty, Ed and Tom (1894)

Hamner, Garvin and Granny (1945)

Maher, Frank and Tom (1902)

Thomas, Bill and Roy (1902)

POSTSEASON

1993 World Series

1. Who did the Phillies play in the 1993 World Series?

2. True or False? This was the first World Series played entirely on artificial surfaces.

3. Who was the only Phillies player on the active roster for both the 1983 and '93 World Series?

4. Who started Game 1 for the Phillies?

5. How many runs did the two teams combine for in Game 4 to set a World Series record?

WALL OF FAME

```
T F V A N R O B E R T S F S O
S H L T D I M H C S S I N N E
G N O B C R A V A T H O E F W
T N E M H A M N E R M E T A Y
Q I I W P U F V N M G R L T C
H K M N O S V L I A O E N A K
T S C S N C O S M H X A R V L
A N G E B U A N S A H L A U E
Y I R N O K B L N A T M L K I
L Z A O O N T D L O I A L O N
O U W J N W E E N I E D E V E
R L C M E R D R J H S D N I E
Y L A H A M I L T O N O P C R
N R U B H S A W O B B X N H G
S P W I L L I A M S A M U E L
```

ALEXANDER
ALLEN
ASHBURN
BOONE
BOWA
BUNNING
CALLISON
CARLTON
CRAVATH
DELAHANTY
ENNIS
GREEN
HAMILTON
HAMNER
JONES
KLEIN
LUZINSKI
MADDOX
MAGEE
MCGRAW
OWENS
ROBERTS
SAMUEL
SCHMIDT
SHORT
SIMMONS
TAYLOR
THOMPSON
VUKOVICH
WILLIAMS

Answers on page 94.

6. True or False? Game 5 was the last postseason baseball game in Veterans Stadium.

7. How many games did the Series go?

8. Which television network carried the Series?

9. Was the payout for each Phillies player share more or less than $100,000?

10. Who was the Series' MVP?

Answers on page 94.

1983 World Series

1. The Series was nicknamed for which interstate highway that connects Philadelphia and Baltimore?

2. The Phillies lost the Series, four games to one. Which game did the Phillies win?

3. Which Phils pitcher was the only one to win a game?

4. Which Phillies player became the second oldest to hit a home run in World Series history?

5. Which Baltimore pitcher became the first to win a Series game in three different decades?

6. Who was the only Phils pitcher to lose two games?

7. Who was the Series MVP?

8. Who was the MLB commissioner who made his final World Series trophy presentation that year?

9. Did the Phillies bat over or under .200 as a team in the Series? Did they score more or less than 10 runs in the five games combined?

10. The crowd of 66,947 in Game 4 at Veterans Stadium was the largest for a World Series game since 1964. Which team had a larger crowd in that 1964 Series?

Answers on page 95.

1980 World Series

1. True or False? The Phillies became the last of the original NL and AL franchises to win a World Series.

2. True or False? This was the first World Series played entirely on artificial turf.

3. Which Phillies pitcher became the first rookie pitcher since 1952 to start Game 1 of the World Series?

4. Who struck out the Royals' Jose Cardenal with two outs and the bases loaded in the bottom of the ninth inning of Game 5 in the Phils' 4-3 win?

5. Who struck out the Royals' Willie Wilson for the final out of Game 6 and the final out of the Series?

6. Who was the official MVP of the Series?

7. Who was the Phillies manager?

8. Who were the three future Hall of Famers who played in the Series?

9. The Phillies and Royals squared off against each other again after the Series on which popular TV game show?

10. Which Phillies pitcher won two games, and which was credited with two saves?

Answers on page 95.

Other Postseasons

1. Which team did the Phillies lose to in the 1915 World Series?

2. Which team did the Phillies lose to in the 1950 World Series?

3. Which team swept the Phils, 3 games to none, in the 1976 NL Championship Series?

4. In 1977, the Phillies won their first postseason game in 62 years. Which team did they beat, and for bonus points, who was the winning pitcher?

5. Which Phillies pitcher won the game and hit a three-run homer in the team's only victory in the 1978 NL Championship Series versus the Dodgers?

6. True or False? The Phillies and Astros played four consecutive extra-inning games in the 1980 NL Championship Series.

7. Who was the Expos pitcher who shut out the Phillies, 3-0, in the deciding game of the 1981 NL Championship Series?

8. Which Phillies slugger hit home runs in three consecutive games to lead Philadelphia over the Dodgers in the 1983 NL Championships Series?

9. Who was the Phils' closer who struck out PH Bill Pecota for the final out in the final game of the 1993 NL Championship Series win over Atlanta?

10. Which Phillies hit back-to-back home runs in Game 1 of the 2007 NL Division Series against Colorado?

Answers on page 95.

RETIRED UNIFORM NUMBERS

In its history, the Philadelphia Phillies have retired seven players' numbers. Some of Major League Baseball's greatest players are on this list, including Mike Schmidt (20), Chuck Klein, Richie Ashburn (1) and pitchers Jim Bunning (14), Robin Roberts (36), Grover Cleveland Alexander and Steve Carlton (32). (The Phillies – along with every other major league team – have also retired No. 42 in honor of Jackie Robinson.)

Klein and Alexander played before there were numbers on the jerseys. Both are National Baseball Hall of Fame members.

In addition, the Phillies honor former greats with a Wall of Fame located at Citizens Bank Park. Thirty former Phillies names are on this Wall along with the names of 25 former Philadelphia A's. Juan Samuel was the last Phillie to join the Wall of Fame, in 2008.

Richie Ashburn

1. Which position did Richie play for most of his Phillies career?

2. Which position did Richie play when he signed his first pro contract in 1945?

3. Within 100, what is his Phillies franchise record for most consecutive games played?

4. Which two NL teams did Richie play for after leaving the Phillies following the 1959 season?

5. True or False? Richie was the NL Rookie of the Year in 1948.

Answers on page 95.

Jim Bunning

1. Which team did the Phillies trade with to obtain Jim in 1963?

2. True or False? Bunning was the first player to pitch for both leagues in the All-Star Game.

3. What was significant about Jim's 4-1 win over Montreal on Apr. 10, 1971?

4. True or False? Jim's perfect game on Father's Day 1964 was the first by an NL hurler in more than 80 years.

5. Which state does Jim represent in the U.S. Senate?

Answers on page 95.

Steve Carlton

1. Who is the only LHP with more career victories than Carlton?

2. Who did the Phillies trade to the Cardinals to obtain Carlton?

3. How many Cy Young Awards did Steve win in his career?

4. True or False? Steve had more than 4,000 strike outs in his major league career.

5. Steve holds the Phillies career record for most wins (241). Who are the only other two LHP with 100+ wins in a Phillies uniform?

Answers on page 96.

Robin Roberts

1. Name two of the three major league teams Robin pitched for after leaving the Phillies following the 1961 season.

2. Which college did Roberts graduate from?

3. True or False? Robin threw complete games in 28 consecutive starts in 1952-53.

4. Name one of the two pitchers he shares the record with for most All-Star Games started.

5. True or False? Robin averaged more than one strikeout per inning pitched with the Phils.

Answers on page 96.

Grover Cleveland Alexander

1. How many victories did Alexander have in his rookie season with the Phils in 1911?

2. True or False? Grover's 16 shutouts in 1916 are still a major league record.

3. Who portrayed Grover in the 1952 motion picture "The Winning Team?"

4. True or False? Grover was the great-grandson of U.S. President Grover Cleveland.

5. Who is the only player in major league history with more career shutouts than Alexander's 90?

Answers on page 96.

Chuck Klein

1. Did Chuck bat right- or left-handed?

2. How many times did he lead the NL in home runs?

3. True or False? Chuck's 44 assists in 1930 are the most by an outfielder in any season since 1900.

4. What number did Chuck wear with the Phillies?

5. True or False? He played in the very first major league All-Star Game in 1933.

Answers on page 96.

UNIFORM NUMBERS

Match these players with the uniform number they wore for most of their Phillies career.

1. Bobby Abreu	a. 4
2. Larry Bowa	b. 6
3. Lenny Dykstra	c. 8
4. Ryan Howard	d. 10
5. Greg Luzinski	e. 11
6. Gary Maddox	f. 14
7. Ryan Madson	g. 16
8. Art Mahaffey	h. 19
9. Tug McGraw	i. 25
10. Cookie Rojas	j. 28
11. Jimmy Rollins	k. 31
12. Pete Rose	l. 38
13. Juan Samuel	m. 45
14. Curt Schilling	n. 53
15. Jim Thome	o. 63

Answers on page 97.

MIKE SCHMIDT

The most successful of all Phillies, third baseman Mike Schmidt spent his entire 18-year career in Philadelphia. A native of Dayton, Ohio, Schmidt joined the team during the 1972 season and led the league in home runs two years later.

Schmidt was key to the Phillies' World Series win in 1980. He racked up the honors that year, as he was named the National League's Most Valuable Player and the World Series MVP. He won his second NL MVP Award the following season and his third in 1986.

Over his career, Schmidt was an All-Star 12 times and led the league in home runs eight times. He was a great defensive player as well, winning 10 Gold Glove Awards for his fielding.

The Phillies retired Schmidt's uniform number (20) in 1990, and he was inducted into the National Baseball Hall of Fame in 1995.

Since his retirement, Schmidt has written books, served as a TV commentator, coached hitting for the Phillies, managed a minor league team, and hosted several successful charity events.

1. Where did Mike attend college?

2. The Phillies selected Mike in the second round of the 1971 draft. Who did the Phillies take with their first round pick that year?

3. How many Gold Gloves did Mike win?

4. True or False? Mike was just the fifth player elected to the Baseball Hall of Fame in his first year of eligibility.

5. When he retired, he ranked third on the NL career home run list. Who were the only NL players ahead of him?

6. True or False? Mike was named the MVP of the 1980 and '83 World Series.

7. What team did Mike manage in 2004?

8. Which defensive positions did Mike play for the Phils in his career?

9. True or False? Schmidt hit into a major league record three triple plays in his career.

10. Mike still hosts an annual event in the Bahamas to raise money for charity. What sport do his guests compete in?

Answers on page 97.

MIKE SCHMIDT

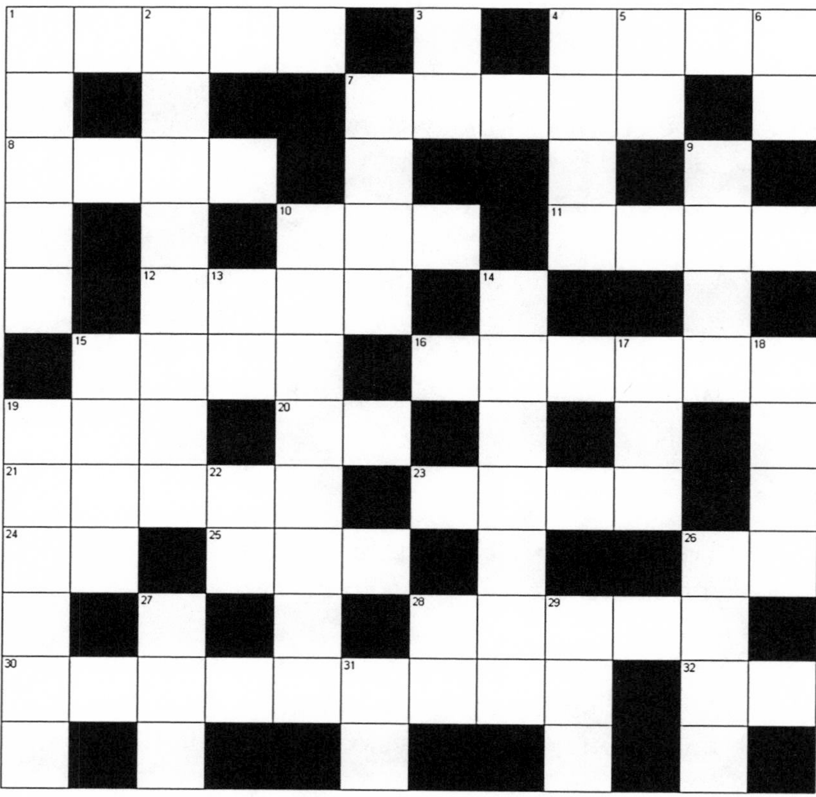

ACROSS

1. Stadium level and 52 playing cards
4. 9-inning contest
7. Type of college exam
8. All tied
10. Boston Bruin great
11. Reverberation
12. Wander
15. Take on in the workplace
16. Home of Fairview HS, Mike's alma mater ☆
19. No. of Gold Gloves won by Schmidt ☆
20. Abreu and Callison's pos.
21. Earnings
23. Michael Schmidt's middle name ☆
24. Movie alien (init.)
25. Female deer
26. Boxing result (abbr.)
28. Former MLB home run

champ

30. Schmidt's usual position ☆
32. Chicago train

DOWN

1. Sleep image
2. Mike's latest book: ___ *the Bases* ☆
3. About 3.14
4. Stadium entry
5. Red Sox and Yankees' affil.
6. Former
7. Schmidt's word of warning after a tee shot ☆
9. College Mike attended ☆
10. Received too many orders
13. Either's partner
14. Site of Mike's annual Winner's Circle Invitational fishing tourney ☆
15. Miami's NBA squad
17. For shame!
18. Roman fiddler
19. Schmidt's uniform no. with the Phillies ☆
22. Phillies Bouchee or Waitkus
26. Leg joint
27. Single or double, e.g.
28. One step below AAA
29. Color on Phillies uniform
31. Scorecard notation for a walk

Answers on page 98.

HITTERS

Mike Schmidt holds practically every career hitting record in Phillies history. But was he the greatest Phillies hitter ever? Probably so, but others could make a strong case for being his equal.

Chuck Klein won the National League Triple Crown in 1933 when he hit .368 with 28 home runs and 120 runs batted in. Klein's career .546 slugging percentage tops Schmidt's .527. Klein's .326 career batting average is also tops among Phillies with multiple seasons.

However, Richie Ashburn batted better than .300 seven consecutive seasons and eight overall. He led the NL twice in hitting. More recently, Ryan Howard has hit for power at a clip exceeding Schmidt's heyday.

If you include the really old-timers, the best hitting outfield in major league history was the 1894 Phillies. Sam Thompson (.404), Ed Delahanty (.400) and Bill Hamilton (.399) combined for a .400 batting average, well ahead of the No. 2 Detroit Tigers' combined average of .380 in 1925.

1. Who holds the Phils record for most hits in a season?

2. Who was the last Phillies player to lead the NL in batting average?

3. Jimmy Rollins holds the franchise record, with 28 lead-off home runs in his career. Who is second on the list, with 14 lead-off HR?

4. Who are the only three Phillies to hit four home runs in a single game?

5. Who were the only two Phils to hit three home runs in a game in the 1990s?

6. Which Phils slugger became the first player in major league history to hit two home runs in the first inning of a game? (Hint: He did it in 1985.)

7. What is the Phillies team record for most home runs in a game?

8. Name one of the two pitchers who hit 11 home runs while playing for the Phils.

9. Who is the only Phils player to hit four grand slam home runs in a season?

10. Since 1913, only one Phillies player has hit three inside-the-park home runs in a season. Who was he?

11. Who holds the Phillies club record for most strikeouts in his career?

12. Who was the Phils hitter who led the club in pinch hits eight times from 1979-88?

13. Who was the last Phillies player to lead the NL in hits in a season?

14. What is the Phillies record for consecutive game hitting streak set by Jimmy Rollins in the 2005-06 seasons?

15. Have the Phils ever scored 20 or more runs in a game?

16. Since 1959, who is the only Phils player to ground into three double plays in one game?

17. True or False? Connie Ryan is the only Phillies player in history with six hits in a game.

18. Who are the only three switch-hitters for the Phillies to hit .300 during a season?

19. Which switch-hitter has the most career hits for the Phillies?

20. True or False? Pete Rose played 163 games for the Phils in 1979.

21. Within 50, how many home runs did Mike Schmidt hit in Veterans Stadium?

22. Who was the Phillies player who hit for the cycle (single, double, triple and home run) in a 2004 game?

23. Who is the only Phils hitter with a career slugging percentage higher than .530?

24. What is Mike Schmidt's club record for most total bases in one game?

25. Who holds the Phillies record for most home runs in a season by a switch-hitter?

Answers on page 98.

BEST OF THE BEST

PHILLIES TOP TEN BATTING AVERAGE, CAREER

1. Billy Hamilton	.360
2. Ed Delahanty	.347
3. Elmer Flick	.344
4. Sam Thompson	.333
5. Chuck Klein	.326
6. Spud Davis	.321
7. Fred Leach	.312
8. Richie Ashburn	.311
9. John Kruk	.309
10. Pinky Whitney	.307

PHILLIES TOP TEN HOME RUNS, CAREER

1. Mike Schmidt	548
2. Del Ennis	259
3. Pat Burrell	251
4. Chuck Klein	243
5. Greg Luzinski	223
6. Cy Williams	217
7. Dick Allen	204
8. Bobby Abreu	195
9. Johnny Callison	185
10. Willie Jones	180

PHILLIES TOP TEN STOLEN BASES, CAREER

1.	Billy Hamilton	508
2.	Ed Delahanty	412
3.	Sherry Magee	387
4.	Jimmy Rollins	295
5.	Jim Fogarty	289
6.	Larry Bowa	288
7.	Bobby Abreu	254
8.	Juan Samuel	249
9.	Roy Thomas	228
10.	Von Hayes	202

PHILLIES TOP TEN PINCH-HITS, CAREER

1.	Greg Gross	117
2.	Tony Taylor	53
3.	Tommy Hutton	52
4.	Tim McCarver	47
5.	Kevin Jordan	45
6.	Ricky Jordan	43
7.	Ruben Amaro, Jr.	37
8.	Dave Philley	37
9.	Jason Michaels	36
10.	John Briggs	35
	Del Unser	35

BEST OF THE BEST

40 HOME RUNS, SEASON

58, Ryan Howard (2006)
48, Mike Schmidt (1980)
48, Ryan Howard (2008)
47, Jim Thome (2003)
47, Ryan Howard (2007)
45, Mike Schmidt (1979)
43, Chuck Klein (1929)
42, Jim Thome (2004)
41, Cy Williams (1923)
40, Chuck Klein (1930)
40, Dick Allen (1966)
40, Mike Schmidt (1983)

WALK-OFF HOME RUNS, CAREER

10, Mike Schmidt
6, Cy Williams
5, Dick Allen
5, Johnny Callison
5, Gavvy Cravath
5, Del Ennis
5, Von Hayes

SHORTSTOPS

B	O	D	I	A	Y	I	E	L	O	T	W	D	C	Q
R	R	W	O	G	R	S	N	I	L	L	O	R	S	I
A	Y	A	R	O	C	I	Y	G	R	E	N	M	A	H
C	M	O	G	D	L	R	A	F	N	Z	E	F	N	Y
E	A	A	G	A	Z	A	L	S	E	A	V	B	D	D
T	M	Q	R	T	N	E	N	D	I	D	E	A	K	E
I	Z	O	L	O	T	E	N	S	S	R	H	N	R	J
R	L	E	S	C	X	A	L	U	C	O	T	C	E	E
W	J	S	H	W	N	L	E	L	H	F	M	R	K	S
I	Y	E	E	R	E	N	P	L	A	A	O	O	C	U
N	R	N	E	T	O	N	P	I	R	L	N	F	O	S
L	I	F	R	H	R	E	O	V	E	E	E	T	T	U
W	A	A	T	Y	N	G	K	A	I	R	Y	K	S	U
F	B	O	W	A	V	X	O	N	N	S	S	O	R	C
D	S	H	U	L	S	W	I	T	T	L	L	E	B	S

ALLEN
AMARO
ARIAS
BANCROFT
BARTELL
BELL
BOWA
BRAGAN
CROSS
DEJESUS
DOOLAN
FERNANDEZ
FLETCHER
GROAT
HAMNER
HULSWITT
IRWIN
JELTZ
KOPPE
MONEY
NEWSOME
PENA
RELAFORD
ROLLINS
SAND
SCHAREIN
STOCKER
SULLIVAN
THEVENOW
THON
WINE

Answers on page 99.

HITTING LEGENDS

ACROSS

2. Holds Phils record for most HR in a season ☆
6. Over act
10. Combine
11. Fired a gun
12. Group of fish
13. Children
15. Pause in the action
16. Earth or Mars, e.g.
19. 1st Phillies player to record 30 HR/30 SB in a season (2001) ☆
22. Pitcher's stat.
23. His 28 leadoff HR are a club record ☆
25. Military store (abbr.)
27. Single-horned African beast
28. Ear of corn protection
30. 1B + 2*2B + 3*3B + 4*HR
31. Direction opp. of WSW
33. Tee shot
34. Mellencamp hit: "Small ___"
36. Finish

39. 1997 NL Rookie of the Year ☆
41. Conceal
42. Hit a record .360 in his Phillies career ☆
43. Word on a door, sometimes
45. Column heading on daily standings
47. Utilize
48. "The Bull" who led the NL in RBI in '75 ☆
51. Indonesian resort island
52. Bother
53. Only player with more than 300 HR in a Phillies uniform ☆
55. Similar to
56. Winning tic-tac-toe play
58. Phils record holder in career doubles and triples ☆
61. Fictional book
62. Player's memento of a World Series title
63. Ave. crosser

DOWN

1. Site of the Rose Bowl
3. "Lefty" who hit .398 to lead NL in 1929 ☆
4. Hit 29 HR as a Phils rookie in 1964 ☆
5. C with 109 RBI in 1992 ☆
6. Phillies Roebuck or Vosberg ☆
7. A small amount
8. Led NL with 47 HR in 2003 ☆
9. RBI, e.g.

Answers on page 100.

13. NL MVP in 1931 and '32☆
14. Bro or sis
16. Bird in a yule pear tree
17. Reach a destination
18. Part of HOMES
19. Led NL in batting avg. in 1955 and '58 ☆
20. Only player to appear in 163 games in one Phillies season ☆
21. Elevator button
24. Crazy (Sp.)
26. T-shirt sz.
29. Leg joint
32. Hometown OF who made club-record $30,000 in 1950 ☆
35. 1st player to hit 40 HR in a season for the Phils (1923) ☆
37. A grand
38. MVP of 1964 major league All-Star Game ☆
40. Hawaiian necklace
44. Ump: ___ ball!
45. Toupee
46. 5-cent pieces
49. House covering, often
50. Dunked breakfast food
51. Had more hits than any switch-hitter in Phils history ☆
54. Portable bed
56. Sturdy tree
57. Wrigley Field wall covering
59. John Kruk's usual pos. ☆
60. Column heading on roster (abbr.)

PITCHERS

The three pitchers Phillies fans consider the greatest of all time are Steve Carlton, Robin Roberts and Grover Cleveland Alexander. Carlton, who pitched for the Phils from 1972-84, won a team-record 241 games and four Cy Young Awards. Roberts won 234 games with 1,871 strikeouts from 1949-60. Alexander won 190 games with 61 shutouts from 1911-17.

Other top pitchers include left-handers Curt Simmons and Chris Short and right-handers Jim Bunning and Curt Schilling. Top relievers include Tug McGraw, Jim Konstanty, Mitch Williams, Jose Mesa, Ron Reed and current closer Brad Lidge.

1. Since 1970, who is the only Phils pitcher to start 40 or more games in a season?

2. Who was the Phils pitcher who won 16 games as a relief pitcher in one season, 1950?

3. Who are the only two Phillies pitchers with 300+ strikeouts in a season?

4. Since 1917, who is the only Phils pitcher with an earned run average of less than 2.00 in a season?

5. Who is the last right-handed pitcher to win 20+ games in a season for Philadelphia?

6. Who was the Phils infielder who pitched a third of an inning in 2002?

7. Which Phils pitcher is the only in recorded history to strike out the side in one inning on just nine pitches? (Hint: It was in 1991.)

8. Which right-handed reliever set the club record by appearing in 90 games in 1987?

9. True or False? A Phillies pitcher once threw 20 innings in one game.

10. Which Phils southpaw gave up a single to the leadoff man, then retired the next 27 batters in a 1953 game?

11. Who was the Phils pitcher who gave up three consecutive home runs to the Mets in a 2007 game?

12. Who set the Phils record for most strikeouts in a game by a right-handed pitcher during the 1961 season?

13. Which Phillies pitcher set a NL record for most strikeouts in a season by a relief pitcher, with 153 in 1970?

14. Who was the Phils pitcher charged with five wild pitches in one game in 1989?

15. Who lost 12 consecutive games during the 1972 season?

16. Who tied the major league record by losing five 1-0 games during the 1967 season?

17. Who set the Phils club record by finishing 313 games in his career?

18. When was the last time the Phils had two pitchers combine to win 40 games in a season? Bonus points if you can name the pitchers.

19. Which three Phillies pitchers won a Gold Glove Award?

20. Who was the only Phils pitcher to win the Baseball Writers Association of America NL Most Valuable Player Award?

21. Besides Steve Carlton (who won four times), who are the only two Phillies pitchers to win the Cy Young Award?

22. Which three Phils relievers have won the NL Reliever of the Year Award (since 1960)?

23. Which Phils pitcher was chosen as the MVP of the NL League Championship Series in 1993?

24. Who was the only Phils pitcher in the 1960s to earn a NL Pitcher of the Month Award?

25. True or False? Chris Short is in the National Baseball Hall of Fame.

Answers on page 100.

PITCHERS

ACROSS

3. Winning pitcher in '94 All-Star Game ☆
6. Birthday party dessert
8. Made certain
11. Pass catching lineman (abbr.)
12. "Tug" ☆
13. Military address
14. Plays jazz
16. Morning hr.
17. Won two games in '08 World Series ☆
19. Vegas numbers
22. Fruit drink
23. Against (abbr.)
26. His No. 36 is retired by the Phillies ☆
27. II x II
28. Stringed orchestral instrument
29. Looks intently
30. Bathroom need, informally
32. Single or double, e.g.

33. Threw a no-hitter in 2003☆
36. Prefix meaning two
38. Your sister's daughters
40. P named in honor of a U.S. president ☆
41. Dodger's home
42. Moved from mound to U.S. Senate ☆
43. Bull (Sp.)
47. Mature
49. Pitcher's hill
50. Kitchen workers
51. Type of Pete Rose slide, often
52. Formal wear

DOWN

1. Israeli city
2. Pitcher's stat.
4. There are 6 per inning
5. Won 115 games for Phils from 1947-60 ☆
6. Behind bars
7. Gold Glove winner in '76 and '77 ☆
9. Had 18 K's in a '65 game☆
10. Fashion designer name
14. Won '87 Cy Young and Fireman of the Year Awards ☆
15. Type of stoves
18. "Lefty" ☆
20. Relief pitcher's primary goals
21. Sweat
24. Set franchise record with 319 K's in '97 ☆
25. Bullfight cheer
27. That is (abbr.)
29. Philly's home st.
31. Hawaiian dish
34. '83 Cy Young Award winner ☆
35. Sub shop
37. Way out
39. '57 NL Rookie of the Year☆
42. Sacrifice attempt
44. Norway king
45. Phils Daal ☆
46. Inquires
48. Laundry detergent name
50. Phils' pitcher Danny (1991-92) pitched in the World Series with Toronto in '93 ☆

Answers on page 101.

BEST OF THE BEST

PHILLIES TOP TEN PITCHING WINS, CAREER

1.	Steve Carlton	241
2.	Robin Roberts	234
3.	Grover Alexander	190
4.	Chris Short	132
5.	Curt Simmons	115
6.	Curt Schilling	101
7.	Charlie Ferguson	99
8.	Al Orth	98
9.	Kid Carsey	95
10.	Tully Sparks	95
	Jack Taylor	95

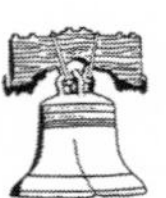

PHILLIES TOP TEN STRIKEOUTS, CAREER

1.	Steve Carlton	3,031
2.	Robin Roberts	1,871
3.	Chris Short	1,585
4.	Curt Schilling	1,554
5.	Grover Alexander	1,409
6.	Jim Bunning	1,197
7.	Curt Simmons	1,052
8.	Brett Myers	936
9.	Randy Wolf	971
10.	Larry Christenson	781

BEST OF THE BEST

NO-HITTERS

Charles Ferguson (1885)
Red Donahue (1898)
Charles Fraser (1903)
Johnny Lush (1906)
Jim Bunning (1964) (perfect game)
Rick Wise (1971)
Terry Mulholland (1990)
Tommy Greene (1991)
Kevin Millwood (2003)

MOST STRIKEOUTS, GAME

18, Chris Short (1965)
17, Art Mahaffey (1961)
16, Steve Carlton (1982)
16, Curt Schilling (1997)
15, Steve Carlton (1981)
15, Curt Schilling (1997)
15, Curt Schilling (1998)
15, Cole Hamels (2007)

BEST OF THE BEST

MOST SAVES, SEASON

45, Jose Mesa (2002)

43, Mitch Williams (1993)

42, Jose Mesa (2001)

41, Brad Lidge (2008)

40, Steve Bedrosian (1987)

38, Billy Wagner (2005)

34, Ricky Bottalico (1996)

34, Ricky Bottalico (1997)

34, Tom Gordon (2006)

32, Heathcliff Slocumb (1995)

MANAGERS

The Phillies have had 51 managers since 1883. Gene Mauch, 1960-68, had the longest tenure, managing 1,331 games. He is also the team's all-time winningest manager, with 645 victories. Close behind is Danny Ozark, the 1970s leader, who won 594 of the 1,105 games he managed. Charlie Manuel has been the Phillies manager since 2005.

The team's first manager, Bob Ferguson, was at the helm for only 17 games, going just 4-13. His replacement, Bill Purcell, had an even lower winning percentage (.165), going 13-68-1.

Twenty men have played and managed the team, starting with Ferguson. The last was Gary Varsho, who played in 1995 and managed (two games) in 2004.

1. Who was the first-year manager for the Phillies when they made their first World Series appearance in 1915?

PHILLIES PHACTS

PHILLIES TOP TEN WINS BY A MANAGER, CAREER

1. Gene Mauch	645
2. Harry Wright	636
3. Danny Ozark	594
4. Jim Fregosi	431
5. Red Dooin	392
6. Eddie Sawyer	390
7. Burt Shotton	370
8. Bill Shettsline	367
9. Charlie Manuel	354
10. Larry Bowa	337

2. Which of these men did not play for and manage the Phillies: Dallas Green, Pat Corrales, Larry Bowa, Pete Rose and Jim Fregosi?

3. Who did Paul Owens replace as manager in midseason of 1983 en route to a World Series berth?

4. True or False? Gene Mauch wound up his major league managing career in 1987 as the winningest manager to have never won a league pennant.

5. What was Danny Ozark's name at birth?

6. Who is the only Phils manager to lead the team to 100+ victories in a season?

7. Which Phillies manager was preceded by John Felske and succeeded by John Vukovich?

8. Which Phillies coach was the team's manager for the final two games of the 2004 season after Larry Bowa was fired?

9. Which school did Terry Francona lead to the 1980 College World Series title as the tournament's Most Outstanding Player?

10. When the Phillies lost nine of their first 13 games in 1991, who did Jim Fregosi replace as manager?

Answers on page 101.

CRYPT-O-ZARK QUOTES

Danny Ozark was manager of the Phillies from 1973-79. He was one of the franchise's most successful managers (594-510), but he's remembered most for his sometimes odd sayings. See if you can decipher the famous Ozark quotes in these cryptograms. Answers are on page 101.

Hints: Every K you see here is actually an A. The code remains the same through all four quotes.

1. "TGTS SKRJZTJS CKU CMI QKOTDBKOT."

2. "CMI ZMVMOKOMJSI KDT ZMVMOZTII."

3. "CJQ MI JFD VJDKZT? VJDKZMOP KO OCMI RJMSO MIS'O K XKYOJD."

4. "CKZX OCMI BKVT MI SMSTOP RTDYTSO VTSOKZ."

MANAGERS

Y	F	F	U	D	R	E	T	D	G	T	O	D	A	L
W	M	R	E	M	M	I	Z	M	R	I	R	W	I	N
F	L	E	T	C	H	E	R	E	N	N	I	K	S	M
G	E	G	N	I	S	L	B	A	I	L	E	E	U	N
L	H	O	M	I	E	O	M	A	S	M	G	R	S	A
W	L	S	U	Y	L	P	R	O	T	H	R	O	M	S
M	I	I	V	F	A	S	N	E	W	A	E	T	I	H
A	W	A	E	H	R	T	T	Y	Y	E	E	N	T	R
N	W	S	C	N	R	A	T	T	Q	W	N	K	H	D
U	O	O	U	M	O	L	N	F	E	I	A	S	G	O
E	B	T	B	Y	C	L	U	C	C	H	E	S	I	O
L	F	I	T	Z	S	I	M	M	O	N	S	M	R	I
K	R	A	Z	O	E	N	O	O	D	N	G	S	W	N
X	M	A	U	C	H	G	H	T	A	V	A	R	C	W
G	G	K	F	E	L	S	K	E	M	O	R	A	N	R

BOWA
CHAPMAN
CORRALES
CRAVATH
DOOIN
DUFFY
ELIA
FELSKE
FITZSIMMONS
FLETCHER
FRANCONA
FREGOSI
GREEN
IRWIN
LEYVA
LOBERT
LUCCHESI
MANUEL
MAUCH
MCINNIS
MORAN
MURRAY
MYATT
NASH
ONEILL
OWENS
OZARK
PROTHRO
SAWYER
SHETTSLINE
SHOTTON
SKINNER
SMITH
STALLINGS
WILHELM
WILSON
WRIGHT
ZIMMER

Answers on page 102.

STADIUMS

They say home is where the heart is, and for Philadelphia Phillies fans, that is Citizens Bank Park.

The Phillies home opened on April 12, 2004 when Philadelphia took on the Cincinnati Reds. The 43,647-seat stadium is on the north side of Pattison Avenue between Citizens Bank Way and Darien Street. The modern facility features three levels – the lower deck, a suite level and the upper deck – and gives fans a fantastic view of downtown Philadelphia.

Citizens Bank Park has a festive atmosphere. Inside the field area, a 50-foot neon Liberty Bell replica swings and rings whenever a Phillie hits a home run. The outfield concourse features Ashburn Alley, an entertainment area with concession stands, picnic areas, views of the field and a team store. The area is named after Richie "Whitey" Ashburn, a former Phillies Hall of Famer and broadcaster. This area pays tribute to the Phillies and includes 10-foot-tall bronze sculptures of Ashburn as well as Phillies greats Mike Schmidt, Steve Carlton and Robin Roberts. There are also granite markers for each Philadelphia All-Star since 1933.

Before moving to Citizens Bank Park, the Phillies spent more than 30 years in Veterans Stadium. The baseball team shared Veterans Stadium with the NFL's Philadelphia Eagles. "The Vet," located at the northeast corner of Broad Street and Pattison Avenue, had a baseball capacity of 56,371. The Phillies played their first game in Veterans Stadium on April 10, 1971, defeating Montreal.

The Vet hosted the 1976 and 1996 Major League Baseball All-Star Games.

In its later years, the stadium was known as one of the worst in the league, mainly due to its problematic Astroturf. The turf was uneven and gapped with visible seams, giving rise to the nickname "Field of Seams."

Connie Mack Stadium (also named Shibe Park), Baker Bowl (also named National League Park and Philadelphia Base Ball Grounds) and Recreation Park have also been home to the Phillies.

Veterans Stadium

1. Veterans Stadium was located at the northeast corner of which two roads?

2. In 1976, Veterans Stadium hosted the All-Star Game, and the Phillies had five players selected for the first time. Name four of those players.

3. Which two out-of-town college football teams played in Veterans Stadium 17 times from 1976-2001?

4. True or False? Veterans Stadium was constructed as a perfect circle.

5. How many seating levels were there at Veterans Stadium?

6. Who hit the longest home run in Veterans Stadium history? (Hint: It was not a Phillies player.)

7. Which team did the Eagles lose to in the NFC Championship Game played on Jan. 19, 2003, in the final football game at the Vet?

8. Which Phillies Hall of Fame pitcher won the first game at Veterans Stadium in 1971 over the Montreal Expos?

9. True or False? The stadium was a tribute to the veterans of the Vietnam War.

10. Which Phillies great flipped the imaginary switch to implode the stadium?

Answers on page 102.

Citizens Bank Park

1. Who threw the first pitch of the first game in the park on Apr. 12, 2004?

2. What is the name of the indoor club area located behind home plate?

3. What is the name of the club located on the second level, between Sections 212 and 232?

4. Which national organization named Citizens Bank Park as America's most vegetarian-friendly ballpark?

5. Who performed the first musical concert at the park, on Aug. 25, 2005?

6. Whose ashes were spread on the pitcher's mound prior to the first World Series game in the park in 2008?

7. Which is farther, the distance from home plate to the left field foul pole or home plate to the right field foul pole?

8. In what year was the ground breaking for the stadium?

9. Who hit the first "walk off" home run for the Phillies in the park?

10. What's the ruling when a ball wedges in the chain link fence in front of the out-of-town scoreboard in right field?

Answers on page 103.

MOST PITCHING APPEARANCES AT CITIZENS BANK PARK, CAREER

155, Ryan Madson

108, Geoff Geary

100, Rheal Cormier

86, Brett Myers

80, Billy Wagner

THE ANSWERS

2008 Players (from pages 10-12)

Hitters: 1. g; 2. k; 3. h; 4. e; 5. f; 6. i; 7. j; 8. d; 9. b; 10. l; 11. n; 12. a; 13. m; 14. c.
Pitchers: 1. c; 2. i; 3. f; 4. h; 5. a; 6. k; 7. b; 8. j; 9. d; 10. e; 11. g.

2008 Players (from pages 14-15)

2008 Season (from page 16)

1. Shane Victorino and Ryan Howard; 2. Cole Hamels (2) and Brett Myers (2); 3. Jamie Moyer, who was 45; 4. Carlos Ruiz (92 games), Chris Coste (69 games) and Lou Marson (1 game); 5. Home (48-33) vs. road (44-37); 6. Florida Marlins on Sept.

19; 7. Jayson Werth; 8. 7 games; 9. 6 games; 10. True; 11. Adam Dunn (122) and Albert Pujols (104); 12. They tied with 78 each; 13. Jamie Moyer; 14. Tim Lincecum (.221); 15. Six straight seasons; 16. True; 17. Jayson Werth (20-for-21) and Jimmy Rollins (47-for-50); 18. 18 straight games; 19. False. They led the NL, but the White Sox had 233 HR in the AL; 20. Jamie Moyer was 10-3; 21. Ryan Howard (.320); 22. True; 23. Kyle Kendrick; 24. Below. The Phils led the NL with a 3.22 bullpen ERA; 25. Above. The Phils were second in the NL with a .253 pinch-hitting batting average.

Ryan Howard (from pages 19-20)

1. Southwest Missouri State University.
2. David Ortiz.
3. Joe DiMaggio, with 167 RBIs in 1937.
4. Ralph Kiner, who hit his 100th HR in his 385th game.
5. James.
6. True. Albert Pujols won the NL MVP award in 2008.
7. False. Hank Sauer of the Reds was leading the NL in HR and RBI at the All-Star break in 1948, but he didn't make the All-Star team.
8. Chuck Klein had four consecutive 30 HR/100 RBI seasons with the Phillies from 1929-32.
9. He has hit .304 against RHP and .231 against LHP.
10. Howard has hit 24 HR against both Atlanta and Washington. Conversely, he's had just one HR against Pittsburgh.

Howard-Do-Ku (from page 20-21)

O	H	A	D	R	W
D	W	R	A	H	O
R	A	D	O	W	H
H	O	W	R	A	D
W	R	O	H	D	A
A	D	H	W	O	R

W	H	D	R	O	A
A	O	R	D	W	H
O	A	W	H	R	D
D	R	H	O	A	W
R	D	A	W	H	O
H	W	O	A	D	R

A	W	O	H	D	R
H	R	D	W	A	O
D	O	H	R	W	A
R	A	W	D	O	H
W	H	A	O	R	D
O	D	R	A	H	W

Jimmy Rollins (from pages 22-23)

1. Second round.
2. Three (2001, '02 and '05). He is a perfect 3-for-3 at the plate in those three games.
3. 39.
4. More than. He hit safely in 38 consecutive games spanning the 2005-06 seasons.
5. False. Rollins has hit three inside-the-park HR.
6. Cincinnati's Barry Larkin won the award in 1995.
7. False. He played second base in one game.
8. The other three were Frank Schulte (Cubs, 1911), Willie Mays (Giants, 1957) and Curtis Granderson (Tigers, 2007).
9. Willie Wilson of the Kansas City Royals had the record, with 705 AB in 1980.
10. Granny Hamner had 61 HR for the Phils from 1944-59.

Chase Utley (from pages 23-24)

1. Chuck Klein (1929-32) and Lefty O'Doul (1929) are the other two.
2. UCLA.
3. True. He was the third Phillie whose first major league hit was a grand slam.
4. Placido Polanco was moved from 2B to 3B to make room for Chase in the line-up.
5. True. He grounded out to end the game versus Atlanta.
6. Jeff Kent (1997-2002) and Charlie Gehringer (1932-36).
7. He turned 30 years old.
8. Chase had a fractured right wrist after being hit by a pitch.
9. True. He hit .312 at home and .285 on the road.

10. The Los Angeles Dodgers.

Charlie Manuel (from pages 25-26)

1. He managed the Cleveland Indians from 2000-02.
2. Danny Ozark led the Phillies to three straight division titles from 1976-78.
3. The Minnesota Twins hired him as a scout in 1982.
4. The Minnesota Twins (1969-72) and Los Angeles Dodgers (1974-75).
5. Billy Martin and Walter Alston.
6. True. Charlie led the league in batting average, home runs and RBI in 1967.
7. Japan League.
8. He bats left-handed.
9. He throws right-handed.
10. Charlie resides at Winter Haven, Fla., in the off-season.

2008 Coaches (from page 27)

1. c; 2. f; 3. b; 4. d; 5. g; 6. e; 7. a.

2008 World Series (from page 28-29)

1. Wednesday; 2. Chase Utley; 3. Cole Hamels; 4. Tropicana Field; 5. Eric Bruntlett; 6. Carlos Ruiz; 7. Carlos Ruiz, Chase Utley and Ryan Howard; 8. Joe Blanton; 9. True, sort of. Due to a rain delay, Game 3 did not end until after midnight, local time, on Oct. 26. Game 4 was played the evening of Oct. 26; 10. The middle of the sixth inning; 11. J.C. Romero was the winner and Brad Lidge got the save; 12. True; 13. The game was televised by FOX with announcers Joe Buck and Tim McCarver; 14. Cole Hamels; 15. The Commissioner's Trophy, and it was made by Tiffany & Co.

Minor Leagues (from page 30)

1. E-b; 2. A-e; 3. C-c; 4. D-a; 5. B-d.

History (from pages 33-36)

1. Tony Taylor; 2. 21 innings in a 1918 game; 3. Pat Gillick; 4. Ruben Amaro Jr.; 5. RF Jayson Werth and 3B Pedro Feliz; 6. Pat Burrell ($14.2M); 7. True; 8. Fred Luderus (1,298 from 1910-20); 9. Shane Victorino in 2006; 10. Bob Boone; 11. Gary Maddox; 12. Darren Daulton; 13. Scott Rolen; 14. Mickey Morandini; 15. Taylor Swift; 16. Bobby Wine; 17. 1978. The Phanatic was named the No. 1 sports mascot by Forbes Magazine in 2008; 18. David Raymond; 19. Harry Kalas. He began announcing for the Phils in 1971; 20. WPHT-AM; 21. Bright House Networks Field; 22. Manny Trillo; 23. Ozzie Virgil Jr.; 24. Ron Reed; 25. John Kruk.

Major League Teams (from page 34)

Rookies (from pages 37-38)

1. Del Ennis; 2. Dick Allen; 3. Willie Montanez (30 HR in 1971); 4. Marlon Anderson in 1998; 5. 103; 6. Juan Samuel in 1984; 7. Jack Baldschun; 8. Ray Culp; 9. Mike Lieberthal; 10. Dick Allen in 1964.

Baseball Hall of Fame (from page 39)

Each of the Hall of Famers listed played with the Phillies.

Who Am I? (from page 40)

Tim McCarver.
Juan Samuel.

What's Your Name? (from page 41)

1. v; 2. f; 3. u; 4. x; 5. e; 6. g; 7. i; 8. b; 9. j; 10. c; 11. t; 12. h; 13. k; 14. n; 15. r; 16. s; 17. w; 18. y; 19. m; 20. q; 21. a; 22. p; 23. d; 24. l; 25. o.

All-Star (from page 42-43)

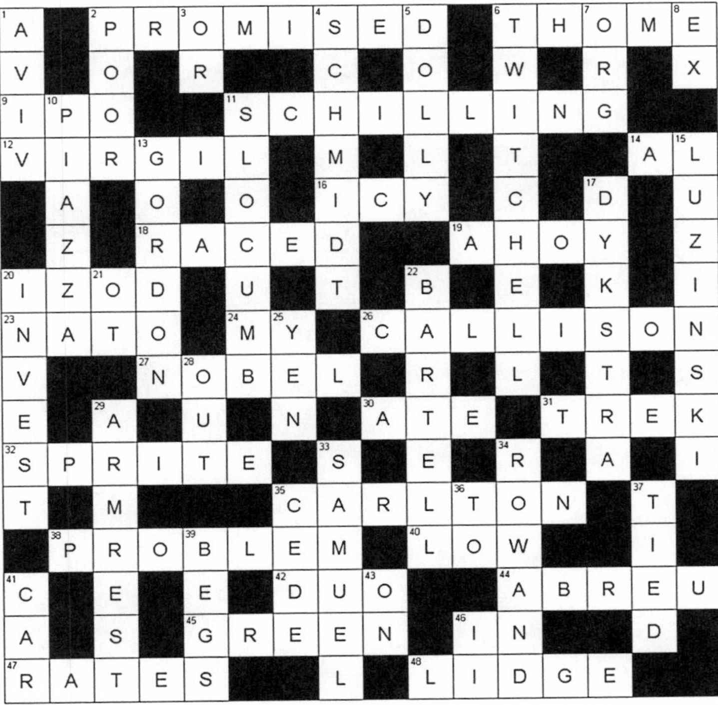

1993 World Series (from pages 44-46)

1. Toronto Blue Jays; 2. False. It was the fourth Series played entirely on artificial surfaces; 3. Larry Anderson; 4. Curt Schilling; 5. 29 (Toronto 15, Philadelphia 14); 6. True; 7. Six; 8. CBS; 9. Less. Each player received $91,222; 10. Toronto's Paul Molitor.

Wall of Fame (from page 45)

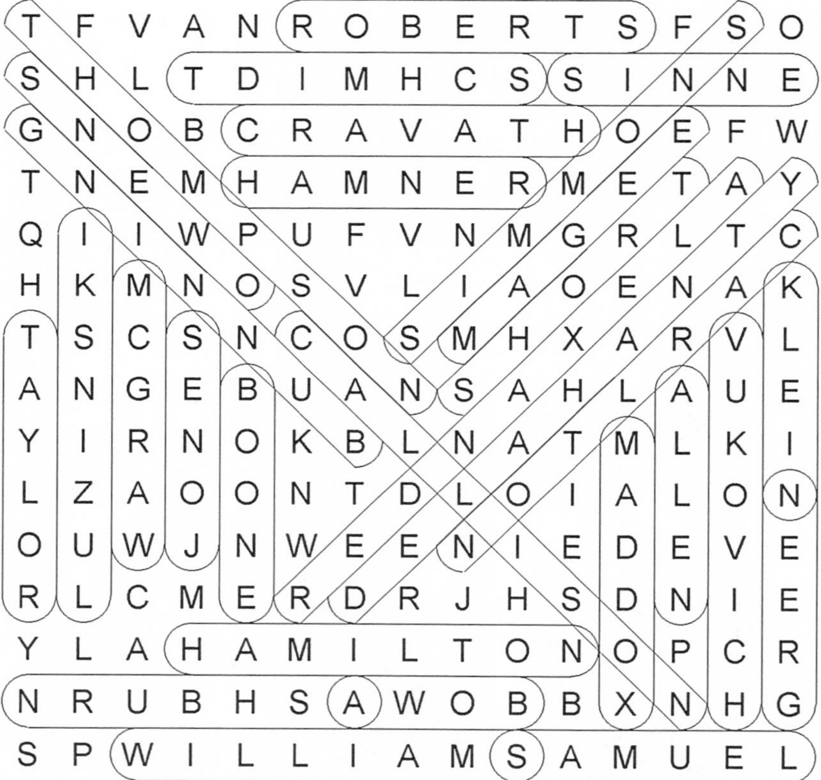

1983 World Series (from pages 46-47)

1. I-95; 2. Game 1; 3. John Denny; 4. Joe Morgan, 40 years old; 5. Jim Palmer; 6. Charles Hudson; 7. Baltimore's Rick Dempsey; 8. Bowie Kuhn; 9. Under—they hit .195. And less than—they scored 9 total runs; 10. New York Yankees.

1980 World Series (from pages 48-49)

1. True; 2. True; 3. Bob Walk; 4. Tug McGraw; 5. Tug McGraw; 6. Mike Schmidt; 7. Dallas Green; 8. Steve Carlton, Mike Schmidt and George Brett; 9. Family Feud. The Phillies won the TV "series," 3-2; 10. Steve Carlton had two wins and Tug McGraw had two saves.

Other Postseasons (from page 49-50)

1. Boston Red Sox, 4 games to 1; 2. New York Yankees, 4 games to 0; 3. Cincinnati Reds; 4. Los Angeles Dodgers, and Gene Garber was the winning pitcher; 5. Steve Carlton; 6. True. The Phillies won the final two contests to win the Series, 3 games to 2; 7. Steve Rogers; 8. Gary Matthews; 9. Mitch Williams; 10. Aaron Rowand and Pat Burrell.

Richie Ashburn (from page 51)

1. Center field.
2. He was a catcher.
3. Richie played in 730 consecutive games from 1950-54.
4. He played for the Cubs (1960-61) and the Mets (1962).
5. True.

Jim Bunning (from page 52)

1. The Phils traded Don Demeter and Jack Hamilton to the Detroit Tigers for Jim and Gus Triandos.
2. True.
3. Jim started and won that game, which was the first played in Veterans Stadium.
4. True. The previous perfect game in the NL had been in 1880.
5. His native Kentucky.

Steve Carlton (from pages 52-53)

1. Warren Spahn had 363 wins, Carlton had 329.
2. Rick Wise, who won 17 games and had a 2.88 ERA in 1971 for the Phils. In 1972, Carlton won a league-high 27 games with a league-best 1.97 ERA in his first season with the Phillies.
3. Four (1972, '77, '80 and '82).
4. True. He had 4,136 in his career that ran from 1965-88.
5. Chris Short (132) and Curt Simmons (115).

Robin Roberts (from page 53)

1. After leaving the Phillies, he pitched with Baltimore (1962-65), Houston (1965-66) and the Cubs (1966).
2. Michigan State University in 1947.
3. True.
4. Lefty Gomez, Don Drysdale and Robin each started five All-Star Games.
5. False. He had 1,871 K in 3,739.1 IP for the Phillies.

Grover Cleveland Alexander (from page 54)

1. He had 28 wins in his first season. That remains a modern day major league record for rookies.
2. True.
3. Ronald Reagan.
4. False. He was just named after the former U.S. president.
5. Walter Johnson had 110 shutouts.

Chuck Klein (from pages 54-55)

1. He batted left-handed.
2. He led the league in HR four times.
3. True.
4. At various times with the Phillies, he wore numbers 1,

3, 8, 26, 29, 32 and 36. That's why the Phillies honored Chuck with the Old English "P" worn by the team during his debut season rather than a number.

5. True. He went on to win the Triple Crown that season.

Uniform Numbers (from page 55)

1. n; 2. d; 3. a; 4. b; 5. h; 6. k; 7. o; 8. j; 9. m; 10. g; 11. e; 12. f; 13. c; 14. l; 15. i.

Mike Schmidt (from page 56-57)

1. Ohio University.
2. Pitcher Roy Thomas from Lompoc, Calif. The Phils traded Thomas in the deal that brought Jim Kaat to Philadelphia. Thomas went on to go 20-11 with seven saves for three major league teams over eight seasons.
3. 10.
4. False. Mike was selected in his first year, but he was the 26th player to enter in his first year of eligibility.
5. Hank Aaron and Willie Mays.
6. False. He was named the MVP of the 1980 Series when he hit .381 with two HR and 7 RBI in 6 games. However, in '83 he was just 1-for-20 (.050) with 6 strikeouts.
7. The Phils' Class A minor league team in Clearwater.
8. He played 2,212 games at third base, 157 games at first base, 24 games at shortstop and 6 games at second base.
9. False. He did not hit into any triple plays in his career, tying the major league mark (with nearly every other player who has ever played) for fewest triple plays hit into.
10. Fishing.

Mike Schmidt (from pages 58-59)

1 D	E	2 C	K	S		3 P		4 G	5 A	M	6 E
R		L			7 F	I	N	A	L		X
8 E	V	E	N		O			T		9 O	
A		A		10 O	R	R		11 E	C	H	O
M		12 R	13 O	V	E		14 B			I	
	15 H	I	R	E		16 D	A	Y	17 T	O	18 N
19 T	E	N		20 R	F		H		S		E
21 W	A	G	22 E	S		23 J	A	C	K		R
24 E	T		25 D	O	E		M			26 K	O
N		27 H		L		28 A	A	29 R	O	N	
30 T	H	I	R	D	31 B	A	S	E		32 E	L
Y		T			B			D		E	

Hitters (from pages 60-63)

1. Lefty O'Doul had 254 hits in 1929; 2. Richie Ashburn who hit .350 in 1958; 3. Juan Samuel; 4. Ed Delahanty, Chuck Klein and Mike Schmidt; 5. Benito Santiago and Bobby Estalella; 6. Von Hayes; 7. Seven, in a 1998 game versus the Mets; 8. Larry Christenson and Rick Wise; 9. Vince DiMaggio in 1945; 10. Dick Allen in 1966; 11. Mike Schmidt with 1,883; 12. Greg Gross; 13. Dave Cash with 213 in 1975; 14. 38 games; 15. Yes, nine times, topped by 26 runs against the Mets in a 1985 game; 16. Johnny Estrada in a 2001 game; 17. True. He had six hits in a game in 1953; 18. Larry Bowa (.305 in 1975), Pete Rose (.331 in 1979 and .325 in 1980) and Gregg Jefferies (.306 in 1995); 19. Larry Bowa with 1,798 hits; 20. True; 21. 265; 22. David Bell; 23. Chuck Klein at .546; 24. 17 (4 HR and 1 1B); 25. Jimmy Rollins with 30 in 2007.

Shortstops (from page 67)

Hitting Legends (from pages 68-69)

P	■	H	O	W	A	R	D	■	E	M	O	T	E	■	T	■	S
A	■	■	D	■	L	■	A	D	D	■	■	A	■	S	H	O	T
S	C	H	O	O	L	■	U	■	■	K	I	D	S	■	O	■	A
A	■	■	U	■	E	■	L	U	L	L	■	■	I	■	M	■	T
D	■	P	L	A	N	E	T	■	■	E	■	A	B	R	E	U	■
E	R	A	■	R	■	R	O	L	L	I	N	S	■	O	■	P	X
N	■	R	■	R	H	I	N	O	■	N	■	H	U	S	K	■	L
A	■	T	■	I	■	E	■	C	■	■	T	B	■	E	N	E	■
■	D	R	I	V	E	■	T	O	W	N	■	U	■	■	E	N	D
T	■	I	■	E	■	C	■	■	I	■	■	R	O	L	E	N	■
H	I	D	E	■	H	A	M	I	L	T	O	N	■	E	■	I	N
O	■	G	■	P	■	L	■	■	L	■	■	■	W	I	N	S	■
U	S	E	■	L	■	L	U	Z	I	N	S	K	I	■	I	■	D
S	■	■	B	A	L	I	■	■	A	■	I	■	G	■	C	■	O
A	N	N	O	Y	■	S	C	H	M	I	D	T	■	A	K	I	N
N	■	■	W	■	O	O	O	■	S	■	I	■	I	■	E	■	U
D	E	L	A	H	A	N	T	Y	■	■	N	O	V	E	L	■	T
■	■	F	■	■	K	■	■	R	I	N	G	■	Y	■	S	T	■

Pitchers (from page 70-72)

1. Steve Carlton (41 in 1972 and 40 in 1973); 2. Jim Konstanty; 3. Curt Schilling (319 in 1997 and 300 in 1998) and Steve Carlton (310 in 1972); 4. Steve Carlton (1.97 in 1972); 5. Robin Roberts (23 in 1955); 6. Tomas Perez; 7. Andy Ashby; 8. Kent Tekulve; 9. True. It's happened three times, the last in 1919; 10. Curt Simmons; 11. Cole Hamels; 12. Art Mahaffey; 13. Dick Selma; 14. Ken Howell; 15. Ken Reynolds; 16. Jim Bunning; 17. Tug McGraw; 18. 1980, Steve Carlton (24) and Dick Ruthven (17); 19. Bobby Shantz (1964), Jim Kaat (1976 and 1977) and Steve Carlton (1981); 20. Jim Konstanty in 1950; 21. John Denny (1983) and Steve Bedrosian (1987); 22. Al Holland (1983), Steve Bedrosian (1987) and Brad Lidge (2008); 23. Curt Schilling; 24. Jim Bunning (June 1964); 25. False.

Pitchers (from pages 74-75)

(1) T	■	■	■	(2) E	■	■	(3) J	(4) O	N	E	(5) S	■	(6) C	A	(7) K	E
(8) E	N	(9) S	U	R	E	(10) D	■	U	■	■	I	■	A	■	A	■
L	■	H	■	A	■	I	■	(11) T	E	■	(12) M	C	G	R	A	W
(13) A	P	O	■	■	(14) B	O	(15) P	S	■	(16) A	M	■	E	■	T	■
V	■	(17) R	O	M	E	R	O	■	(18) C	■	(19) O	D	D	(20) S	■	(21) P
I	■	T	■	■	D	■	T	■	A	■	N	■	■	(22) A	D	E
(23) V	(24) S	■	(25) O	■	(26) R	O	B	E	R	T	S	■	(27) I	V	■	R
■	(28) C	E	L	L	O	■	E	■	L	■	■	(29) P	E	E	R	S
■	H	■	E	■	S	■	L	■	(30) T	(31) P	■	A	■	S	■	P
(32) H	I	T	■	(33) M	I	L	L	W	O	O	(34) D	■	(35) D	■	(36) B	I
■	L	■	(37) E	■	A	■	I	■	(38) N	I	E	C	E	(39) S	■	R
(40) A	L	E	X	A	N	D	E	R	■	■	N	■	(41) L	A	■	E
■	I	■	I	■	■	■	S	■	(42) B	U	N	N	I	N	G	■
■	N	■	(43) T	(44) O	R	(45) O	■	■	U	■	Y	■	■	F	■	(46) A
(47) A	G	(48) E	■	L	■	(49) M	O	U	N	D	■	(50) C	O	O	K	S
■	■	R	■	A	■	A	■	■	T	■	■	O	■	R	■	K
(51) H	E	A	D	F	I	R	S	T	■	(52) T	U	X	E	D	O	S

Managers (from pages 79-81)

1. Pat Moran; 2. Pete Rose and Jim Fregosi; 3. Pat Corrales; 4. True. He won 1,902 games to rank 8th on the major league career list; 5. Daniel Leonard Orzechowski; 6. Danny Ozark, who led the team to 101 wins in both 1976 and '77; 7. Lee Elia; 8. Gary Varsho; 9. University of Arizona; 10. Nick Leyva.

Crypt-O-Zark Quotes (from page 81)

1. "EVEN NAPOLEON HAD HIS WATERGATE."
2. "HIS LIMITATIONS ARE LIMITLESS."
3. "HOW IS OUR MORALE? MORALITY AT THIS POINT ISN'T A FACTOR."
4. "HALF THIS GAME IS NINETY PERCENT MENTAL."

Managers (from page 82)

Y F F U D R E T D G T O D A L

W M R E M M I Z M R I R W I N

F L E T C H E R E N N I K S M

G E G N I S L B A I L E E U N

L H O M I E O M A S M G R S A

W L S U Y L P R O T H R O M S

M I I V F A S N E W A E T I H

A W A E H R T T Y Y E E N T R

N W S C N R A T T Q W N K H D

U O O U M O L N F E I A S G O

E B T B Y C L U C C H E S I O

L F I T Z S I M M O N S M R I

K R A Z O E N O O D N G S W N

X M A U C H G H T A V A R C W

G G K F E L S K E M O R A N R

Veterans Stadium (from page 84-85)

1. Broad Street and Pattison Avenue; 2. Bob Boone, Larry Bowa, Dave Cash, Greg Luzinski and Mike Schmidt; 3. Army and Navy; 4. False. It's oval design was known as an "octorad"; 5. Seven, numbered from 100 Level to the infamous 700 General Admission Level for some of the team's most die-hard (and vocal) fans; 6. Willie Stargell; 7. Tampa Bay Buccaneers; 8. Jim Bunning; 9. True, but only partially. The stadium was named by the Philadelphia City Council to honor the veterans of all wars; 10. Greg Luzinski.

Citizens Bank Park (from pages 85-86)

1. Randy Wolf; 2. The Diamond Club; 3. The Hall of Fame Club; 4. People for the Ethical Treatment of Animals (PETA); 5. Jimmy Buffett and the Coral Reefer Band; 6. Tim McGraw spread a handful of ashes from his father, Tug McGraw; 7. Right field is 330 feet, left field is 329 feet; 8. The official ground breaking was June 28, 2002; 9. Doug Glanville, on Apr. 18, 2004, against Montreal; 10. It's a ground rule double.

BIBLIOGRAPHY

Books

2008 Phillies Media Guide. Philadelphia Phillies: Philadelphia.

Clayton, Skip. *50 Phabulous Phillies.* 2000. Sports Publishing, Inc.: Champaign, IL.

Jordan, David M. *Occasional Glory: The History of the Philadelphia Phillies.* 2003. McFarland & Company: Jefferson, NC.

Orodenker, Richard. *The Phillies Reader: A Rich Collection of Baseball Literature That Chronicles The Dramatic History of the Philadelphia Phillies*. 2005. Temple University Press: Philadelphia.

Thorn, John; Palmer, Pete; Gershman, Michael; Silverman, Matthew; Lahman, Sean; Spira, Greg. *Total Baseball: The Official Encyclopedia of Major League Baseball*. 2001. Total Sports: Kingston, NY.

Westcott, Rich. *Tales From the Phillies Dugout*. 2003. Sports Publishing, Inc.: Champaign, IL.

Westcott, Rich and Bilovsky, Frank. *The Phillies Encyclopedia*. 2004. Temple University Press: Philadelphia.

Web Sites

Major League Baseball Statistics:
www.baseball-reference.com

Philadelphia Phillies Official Site:
www.philadelphiaphillies.com

Society for American Baseball Research:
www.sabr.org

Wikipedia: www.wikipedia.org